Books by the author:

The Lost Book of Life: New & Selected Poems for adults, 50-year retrospective of 235 poems (U of Alabama Press) 2026

The Very Hungry Caterpillar's First Poems with art by Eric Carle (Random House) 2026

Southern Bred: A Memoir of Gothic Poems for adults (Central Ave/Simon & Schuster) 2025

Kids Love Coins: An Introduction to Coin Collecting (Whitman) 2025

Sweet Dreams: Moon Poems for Bedtime (Schiffer) 2025

Bound to Dream: An Immigrant Story (Schiffer) 2024

The Magic Box: A Book of Opposites (Schiffer) 2024

The Father Goose Treasury of Poetry for Children: 101 Favorite Poems (Schiffer) 2023

Strange Unusual Gross & Cool Animals (Simon & Schuster) 2023

Little Hearts: Finding Hearts in Nature (Red Comet Press) 2022

Fetch Cat Fetch (Schiffer) 2022

Love Is Everything (Schiffer) 2021

A Poem Is A Firefly (Schiffer) 2021

The Truth About Trees (Negative Capability Press) 2021

Artwords: Artists & Poets: Portraits in Verse (Resource Publications) 2021

Once Upon Another Time (Beaming Books) 2020

Illusions: Poetry & Art for the Young at Heart (Resource Publications) 2019

Dear Poet: Notes to a Young Writer (Resource Publications) 2019

Stones: The Collected Short Poems of Charles Ghigna (Canopic Press) 2019

Alabama: My Home Sweet Home (Whitman) 2018

The Night the Forest Came to Town (Orca) 2018

Puns Not Guns

~Humor~

Charles Ghigna

Livingston Press
The University of West Alabama

Copyright © 2025 Charles Ghigna
All rights reserved, including electronic text
ISBN 13: trade paper 978-1-60489-392-2
ISBN 13: e-book 978-1-60489-393-9
ISBN 13: hardcover 978-1-60489-394-6

Library of Congress Control Number:
2025943307

Typesetting and page layout: Kelly West
Proofreading: Trinity Cates, Kelly West

Cover art: John Caldwell

This is a work of fiction. Any resemblance
to persons living or dead, events, or locales
is coincidental.
Livingston Press is part of
The University of West Alabama,
and thereby has non-profit status.
Donations are tax-deductible.

~ Contents ~

I. POLITICS
Accident Prone	18
Primary Concern	19
Dispose All	20
The Passing of an Error	21
Candid Dates	22
Political Draw	23
Wealthiest Nation?	24
Social Security?	25
Ewe Lie	26
Uncommon Sense	27
Nothing But the Truth	28
No Comment	29
Act of Congress	30
Mathemagicians	31
Capitol Punishment	32
Congress Shoots the Bull	33
Gun Control	34
Boss Art	35
Not Another Meeting!	36
CNNundated	37
Headline News Worthy?	38
No Escapism	39
Remotely Sane	40
Govern Meant	41
Ballot Boxing	42

II. MONEY
Profit of Doom	44
Money Magic	45
CD or Not CD	46
Warrant Tease	47

Insecurity Guard	48
Poor Reader	49
Wealthy and Wise	50
Living Small	51
Stocks and Bondage	52
Family Prophet	53
Budge It	54
Money Shrinks	55
Dough Cart	56
License Lineup	57
Life or Death Insurance	58
Gas Who	59
Mane Man	60
Expensive Trash	61
Miser Able	62
Bathing Suitors	63
Trip Tip	64
Money Talks	65
College Daze	66
Father of the Bride	67

III. MARRIAGE

Presents of Mind	70
Mister Meaner	71
Appraise Worthy	72
Flee Market	73
Artifacts and Fiction	74
Know Promises	75
House Rules	76
Matrimonial Math	77
Perfect Pair	78
The Perfect Union	79
Date Your Mate	80
Hug of War	81
Passion's Paradox	82
Fame Us	83

IV. FAMILY

Rhythm and Blues Method	86
Light Wait	87
Rain Dear	88
Sound Effects	89
Family Vacation	90
Surf Bored	91
Holiday Presence	92
Neat Toys	93
Cabbage Patched	94
The Pediatrician	95
Organized Fun?	96
School Daze	97
The Sweetest Sound	98
Madras or Mattress?	99
Teenage Sage	100
All Shook Up	101
New Fall Fashions	102
Driving Lesson	103
Perpetual Motion	104
Sum Problem	105
Algebra Test Anxiety	106
Blast Off!	107
Muse Sick	108
Son Glasses	109
Mixed Emotions	110
Know Respect	111
Horse Play	112
No Kidding	113
Happy New Year!	114
In Specter	115
Family Reunion	116

V. FOOD & DRINK

Food Fare	118
Bon Appétit — Y'all	119
Lunch Bunch	120

See Food	121
Fasting	122
Starting Next Sundae	123
Sell You Lite	124
Snack Attack	125
Frankly Speaking	126
Steaks Alive!	127
Eggsactly	128
For Butter or Worse	129
Raw Oysters	130
Cereal Killer	131
Dinner Belle	132
Caffeine Kick	133
Air Apparent	134
All Bottled Up	135
Gulable	136
Insight Full	137

VI. HEALTH & FITNESS

The Cold Facts	140
Witch Doctor	141
Owe Well	142
Pet A Cure	143
Pet Peeved	144
Drugged	145
Flu Bugged	146
No It All	147
Medicine Man	148
Waist Full Thoughts	149
No Sweat	150
Sail On	151
Know Sweat	152
The Price of Perspiration	153
SPAtacular	154
The Era of Our Ways	155
Salt Shaker	156
Heart Throb	157

Bored Walk	158
Board Stiff	159
Body and Soil	160
Battle Fatigue	161
Healthy Kick Stand	162
Hexercise	163
Health Food	164
No Weigh	165
Fat Free Advice	166
Nutty Professors	167
Cultured Yogurt	168
Fat Chance	169
Hope Full	170
Food for Thought	171
New Age	172
Fiscal Fitness	173
No Funny Bones About It	174

VII. SPORTS & RECREATION

Golfing Accident	176
Commit Tee Meeting	177
Spare Me	178
Bowling Instructions	179
Boxing Lesson	180
TV Wrestling	181
Head Way	182
Cast of Thousands	183
To Yacht or Not	184
Chess Nut	185

VIII. THE ARTS

Art	188
Choice Art	189
Artfelt Emotion	190
Heart Art	191

Art Show in the Park	192
Staid of the Art	193
Art Eyes	194
A Good Impression	195
Music Matters Phantom of the Opry	196
All That Jazz	197
Jazz Magician	198
Another Pointe of View	199
Ergo Libretto	200
Of Chorus	201
Paint the Sunset	202

IX. LITERATURE

Nevermore	206
Waste Land	207
A Thank You Note to Ogden Nash	208
Musery Love Company	209
Literary Profits	210
The Happy Hypist	211
Busted Bard	212
Re-Verse	213
Stroke of Genius	214
Silent Echoes	215
Writer's Block	216
Poetry Is Not	217
Double Vision	218
Choice Language	219
Suitable Language	220
Book Stand	221
Royal Reader	222
A Novel Idea	223
eBook	224
Light Verse	225
Verse Case Scenario	226
Oh What the Hack	227
It Could Be Verse	228
Write Walking	229

X. SCIENCE & NATURE

Science Faction	232
Sunsational	233
Hay Feverish	234
Wysteria	235
Spring Training	236
Pollen Nation	237
Roadside Flowers	238
Petal Pushers	239
Lawn Hot Summer	240
Summerize	241
Rain Checked	242
The Firefly	243
The Brightest Planet	244
UFO or UAP?	245
Plan It Earth	246
Land Grab	247
The Price of Emission	248
Neil Armstrong	249
Star Attraction	250
Lighten Up	251
It's All Relative	252
The Happy Pessimist	253

XI. TECHNOLOGY

Virtual Reality	256
Old Software	257
PC or Not PC	258
My Cussed Computer	259
Computer Eyes	260
Garden of Eden	261
Deus Ex Machina	262
Know Joke	263
Phone Tag	264
Listen Hear	265
Bar Coded	266
No Cause for Alarm	267

XII. FAITH & INSPIRATION

The Art of Start	270
Blind Faith	271
In Sight	272
Religion	273
Reformation	274
Moving Sermon	275
The Power of Patience	276
Rare Dessert	277
Earth Bound	278
Conscience	279
The Right Angle	280
The Right Touch	281
All the World's a Stage	282
Secrets Are Gossip	283
Mighty Secret	284
Pair Annoyed	285
Light View	286
Jacob's Ladder	287
Unbeaten Path	288
Dalai Lama	289
Proof Positive	290
Tears of Joy	291
Real Quack	292
Mind Bending	293
Light Show	294
Living in the Past	295
The Present	296
The Sell-Us-A-Dream Prophecy	297
Soothsayer or Truthsayer?	298
Life's an Illusion	299
Dream Land	300
Reality Check	301
Double Departure	302

*for Debra
from her Silly Goose
and in loving memory of
Richard Armour*

Puns Not Guns

I. *Politics*

Accident Prone

Most accidents occur at home,
A very simple truth.
But many more also occur
Inside the voting booth.

Primary Concern

We take a chance and cast our vote
And then we wait and see.
No wonder we all feel just like
We played the lottery.

Dispose All

We only get to vote for one,
But in our own defense,
We'd like to know how many we're
Allowed to vote against.

The Passing of An Error

Our past mistakes may come and go,
Though some are prone to stay.
A lesson that we fail to learn—
Until election day.

Candid Dates

Don't be too quick to judge them by
The fanfare they receive.
They are well-liked wherever they go—
Especially when they leave.

Political Draw

Politicians often dwell
Inside their own delusions.
Every time they get the facts,
They draw their own confusions.

Wealthiest Nation?

They say we are the wealthiest,
A message I don't get.
How can we be the wealthiest
When we're so deep in debt?

Social Security?

The government has turned our funds
Into a big uncertainty.
Retirement has now become
Our social insecurity.

Ewe Lie

The candidates are telling lies.
But they will cause no harm.
For when they try to pull the wool—
We recognize their yarn.

Uncommon Sense

Do not let ideology
Get in the way of facts.
Let common sense serve as your guide
When intolerance attacks.

Nothing But the Truth

Journalists are those who put
The truth where it belongs.
They strive to help us see the light
By writing all our wrongs.

No Comment

Congress thinks that double-talk
Will make their speeches sing.
They call themselves a statesman,
But they rarely state a thing.

Act of Congress

Congress tries to keep control
Of all the power it can get.
It has control of everything—
Except the rising debt.

Mathemagicians

Each time the Congress does their math
The one thing that I fear
Is how they think the deficit
Will simply disappear.

Capitol Punishment

Our legislature is fair game.
Their antics are abundant.
No wonder jokes about them seem
To always be redundant.

Congress Shoots the Bull

Gun control is in debate.
Congress tries its luck,
But all they do is shoot the bull
Before they pass the buck.

Gun Control

To keep your gun under control
One item should be noted.
Check first to see that you are sure
Its owner isn't loaded.

Boss Art

Executive ability
Is quite an art, it's true.
The art of taking credit for
The work the others do.

Not Another Meeting!

Committee meetings often run
From silly to sublime.
Although we keep the minutes
We waste hours at a time.

CNNundated

We've all become so hooked on news.
We cannot go to bed.
We're all afraid we might miss what's
No sooner done than said.

Headline News Worthy?

"The more you know, the less you fear"
Is what we used to say—
Till we turned on the cable news
And watched in fear all day!

No Escapism

So many violent movies!
Sometimes it's hard to choose.
If all we want is violence—
We'd watch the evening news.

Remotely Sane

If politics has got you down,
Don't sit around and scoff.
Just cast your vote for the remote—
And turn the TV off.

Govern Meant

Government—
The great provider.
Politics—
The great divider.

Ballot Boxing

Exercise
Your right to vote.
If you win—
Please don't gloat.

II. Money

Profit of Doom

Cable news is cashing in
On headlines full of fear.
They're making money making us
Think Armageddon's here!

Money Magic

Money is a magic wand.
No one can understand it.
Not only is it changing hands,
It changes those who hand it.

CD or Not CD

Interest rates are dropping.
I fear what lies ahead.
Instead of rolling over,
My CD's playing dead.

Warrant Tease

The salesman says the warranty
Will soothe my heart's desires.
He knows the thing won't break until
My warranty expires.

Insecurity Guard

The watchman at our local bank
Is often found reclining.
Whatever it is that makes him tick
Is in need of rewinding.

Poor Reader

Those How-To-Get-Rich books today
Are such a contradiction.
Bookstores ought to shelve them all
Among their works of fiction.

Wealthy and Wise

Achieving wealth is difficult
Without some sacrifice.
Remember that you can't get rich
Until you pay the price.

Living Small

Some folks get a extra charge
At what they call "living large."
That never bothered me at all.
I'm just happy "living small."

Stocks and Bondage

Beware of buying stocks and bonds
Just because they're cheap
Or you may soon become just like
The companies you keep.

Family Prophet

If stocks and bonds have got you down,
Check out your kids' concerns.
Invest in balls and boomerangs—
They give the best returns.

Budge It

We figured out our problem
On our brand new balance sheet.
Our budget would be balanced
If we did not have to eat.

Money Shrinks

Before you try psychiatry
Be certain that you are
Prepared to spend more on a couch
Than you did on your car.

Dough Cart

The most expensive vehicle
Costs nothing at the start,
But it takes lots of money
To drive a grocery cart.

License Lineup

My driver's license photo looks
Like I am doing time.
With what they charged to shoot my mug,
It really was a crime.

Life or Death Insurance

The fine print on my policy
Is giving me some doubt.
I hope it pays, but I am not
Dying to find out.

Gas Who

I pull up to the cheaper pump
To save another dime.
Is premium worth all that much?
Your gas is good as mine.

Mane Man

Instead of fancy hair salons
That flaunt their savoir-faire,
I finally found a barbershop
That simply cuts my hair.

Expensive Trash

Recycled paper puzzles me,
At least that's what I've found.
Why do we pay so much for it
The second time around?

Miser Able

A penny. A quarter.
A nickel. A dime.
While saving his money
He spent all his time.

Bathing Suitors

The cost goes up. The size goes down.
Each summer it's a test
To find the bravest one of all—
Who's paying more for less.

Trip Tip

When packing for a trip abroad,
I know this may sound funny.
Pack half the clothes you think you need—
And twice as much the money.

Money Talks

Money's never mentioned
When speaking of romance,
But say the word "divorce"
And you're talking high finance.

College Daze

The bill from college came today
For all our children's fees.
As parents we are doomed to grow
Much poorer by degrees.

Father of the Bride

His savings spent
On her wedding day,
Yet he reads in the paper
He "gave her away."

III. Marriage

Presents of Mind

To keep a happy marriage strong
These thoughts you must engage,
Remember your wife's birthday—
But forget to say her age.

Mister Meaner

She used her love and kindness
To help me mend my ways.
The only crime I now commit
Is holding her for days.

Appraise Worthy

My wife's an antique connoisseur.
Appraising is her thing.
Every time she looks at me
She wonders what I'd bring.

Flee Market

An acre and a half of junk.
Who could ask for more?
My wife searches for rare antiques—
While I search for the door.

Artifacts and Fiction

"Antique" is such a magic word.
It changes what we see
From being just a throwaway
Into a filigree.

Know Promises

Las Vegas lets us gamble more
Than any place allows.
Roulette and dice and slot machines—
And wedding chapel vows.

House Rules

Most marriages these days will last
(If you should ask most any spouse)
Directly in proportion to
The distance from your in-laws' house.

Matrimonial Math

The odds of staying married rise
With every "I love you."
The sum of these three little words?
One plus one is true.

Perfect Pair

We often seem to disagree
On almost every fact.
We both agree on only this—
Opposites attract.

The Perfect Union

Every day — a brand new start.
Every night — a brand new dream.
Marriage is the best of both.
Two as one — the perfect team.

Date Your Mate

If conversations start to sound
Like you may be debating,
It's time to take your mate out for
Some good old-fashioned dating.

Hug of War

The war of words will end in peace
If both sides use their charms.
When all is finally said and done,
It's time to take up arms.

Passion's Paradox

An empty heart is heavy.
I know that to be true.
My heart is always lightest
When I fill it full of you.

Fame Us

My fifteen minutes worth of fame
Has lasted all my life.
It happens every time I hear
"I love you" from my wife.

IV. Family

The Rhythm and Blues Method

Timing is important
When planning to have kids.
It's not the dos and don'ts that count.
It's the counting of the dids.

Light Wait

At night a toddler's weight will jump.
Sometimes their weight will leap—
Each time we carry them to bed
When they are fast asleep.

Rain Dear

She likes to walk out in the rain
No matter warm or cold.
She lets us know that life's a gift—
She's only three years old.

Sound Effects

Our five-year-old makes lots of noise
With every deed and word.
Unlike the kids of long ago,
He's always seen — and heard.

Family Vacation

The dough we spent on Disney World
We could have saved instead.
The ride the kids remember most
Was jumping on the bed.

Surf Bored

We took the kids down to the beach.
They couldn't wait till dark
So they could leave the beach and play
At the amusement park.

Holiday Presence

A fortune for the latest toys
From bicycles to Lego blocks.
We could have saved a lot this year—
The kids prefer the cardboard box.

Neat Toys

The biggest-selling toys next year,
If I could have my say,
Would be the ones invented
That put themselves away.

Cabbage Patched

Those cubby little cabbage dolls—
Is it against the law
To stuff them in the Cuisinart
And make them into slaw?

The Pediatrician

The waiting room is full of noise.
The doctor shows complaisance
Though he's the one who always has
Such very little patients.

Organized Fun?

Soccer, baseball, scouts and camp,
Piano and ballet,
We've scheduled all our kids so much
They don't have time to play.

School Daze

School days are the happiest
That we will ever know—
Especially when all our kids
Are old enough to go.

The Sweetest Sound

The sound of summer fades away.
The breeze of autumn sings.
The sweetest sound we parents hear
Is when the school bell rings.

Madras or Mattress?

The kids are getting dressed for school.
At least that's what they said.
The clothes we paid a fortune for
Look like an unmade bed.

Teenage Sage

How can it be that we know more
The less we've lived and seen?
Just ask the wisest of us all—
The one who's just thirteen.

All Shook Up

Our daughter has a boyfriend.
She says he's her devotion.
Her constant state of being now—
Perpetual emotion.

New Fall Fashions

The retro look is in again.
There really is no doubt.
Teens are choosing what is in
By wearing what is out.

Driving Lesson

I taught my daughter how to drive.
She finally got it right.
She goes on green and stops on red—
And brakes when I turn white.

Perpetual Motion

A motion that's perpetual
They say cannot be done,
But they would quickly change their minds
If they could see my son.

Sum Problem

The boy disrupted class again.
He had a math attack.
He may not know just how to add—
But he can sure distract.

Algebra Test Anxiety

The test makes him a nervous wreck.
He fears each new equation.
Instead of staying cool and calm
He writhes to the occasion.

Blast Off!

Our son's a heavy metal fan.
He likes a lot of bass.
Each time he turns the volume up
We enter louder space.

Muse Sick

Music is a calming force
That makes our troubles cease.
It soothes the very soul of all—
Except the teenage beast.

Son Glasses

Our son has donned his "shades" again.
His steps are rather slight.
Just one of many side effects
Of looking cool at night.

Mixed Emotions

Ambivalence is best defined
Perhaps in this small way.
In sex ed class our son received
His first and only "A."

Know Respect

Kids won't ask their parents
For advice they need to know.
Instead of "Where did I come from?"
They tell us where to go.

No Kidding

To make your children disappear
And wonder where they hid
Just start a conversation with
"When I was just a kid…"

Horseplay

Unbridled youth is spirited.
It will not be confined—
Until it learns that horse sense lives
Inside a stable mind.

Happy New Year!

The party's lasting way past dawn.
Our house looks like a blur.
We made each guest feel right at home—
That's where we wish they were.

In Specter

I never did believe in ghosts
Or of their strange communion—
That is until I went to my
First family reunion.

Family Reunion

We used to gather once a year.
We all were quite a clan.
Now I miss those gatherings—
As often as I can.

V. Food & Drink

Food Fare

A restaurant choice?
Take my advice.
The lower the lights,
The higher the price.

Bon Appétit — Y'all

To turn your low-cal lunch into
A fancy French soirée
Just cut your carrots into sticks
And call them crudités.

Lunch Bunch

Gossip. Eat.
Repeat.
Chatter
Makes me fatter.

See Food

A mirror in the dining room.
No longer can I cheat.
Instead of endless diets—
I'm watching what I eat.

Fasting

I'm fasting very slowly
Every day and night.
I take my time at every meal
And fast between each bite.

Starting Next Sundae

The urge to diet comes and goes
Until it's finally gone.
It's what we all keep putting off
While we keep putting on.

Sell You Lite

We buy the pricey low-cal food
At the Whole Food store.
Although we get a whole lot less—
We pay a whole lot more.

Snack Attack

We sneak another midnight snack
And think no one will know it.
But those who don't count calories
Have figures that will show it.

Frankly Speaking

The dog is known as man's best friend,
No matter who recites it.
The hot dog though is friendlier—
It feeds the hand that bites it.

Steaks Alive!

The vegetarian enjoys
Dining out for fun.
When asked how she would like her steak—
She tells them on the run.

Eggsactly

Of all the foods
We like to eat,
A scrambled egg
Is hard to beat.

For Butter or Worse

When it comes to butter taste,
The cows, of course, still win it.
Unlike their rival margarine
We know what they put in it.

Raw Oysters

There they sit upon their shell
Looking like — I'll never tell.
No heads, no eyes, just gobs of goo.
Swallow fast — and please don't chew.

Cereal Killer

We bought a healthy cereal.
It looks like little rocks.
It has a ton of fiber
And tastes like the cardboard box.

Dinner Belle

To get us all to clean our plates,
Mother made a pact.
Unless we finished everything—
Next day we'd get it back.

Caffeine Kick

Coffee gives you quite a kick.
It gets you out of bed.
But miss a day or two of brew—
It kicks you in the head.

Air Apparent

We wonder where the fresh air went.
Did we somehow misplace it?
Not only do we see the sky,
Some days we also taste it.

All Bottled Up

Bottled water is the rage
But soon we should beware
The only thing that's fit to breathe
Is freshly bottled air.

Gulpable

We buy our bottled water 'cause
We choose to disbelieve
That Evian spelled in reverse
Suggests we're all naive.

Insight Full

It's true that glasses quickly change
Our vision every time,
Especially when they are filled
With after dinner wine.

VI. Health & Fitness

The Cold Facts

"Virus" is a Latin word
That doctors won't define
Because they know the meaning is
"Your guess is good as mine."

Witch Doctor

So many doctors nowadays.
Each has a specialty.
How do we know which one to call?
That's what's ailing me.

Owe Well

I'm getting sicker every day,
But not from all my ills.
It's from the stress of worrying
About my doctor bills.

Pet A Cure

If you're feeling lonely
There is no need to fret,
Try a little furry friend—
Take home a homeless pet.

Pet Peeved

They said a pet would help relieve
My stress with every hug,
But my new puppy just relieved
His stress upon my rug.

Drugged

Beware prescription drugs
Whenever you detect
The endless list of things
That are a side effect.

Flu Bugged

The only thing worse
Than getting the flu?
The endless advice
Your friends give you.

No It All

A simple health plan that will work
To help get out the bugs?
It's obvious to those who "no"—
No smokes, no booze, no drugs.

Medicine Man

Beware the dermatologist
Whose specialty is rash
For he knows how to quickly turn
Your scratch into his cash.

Waist Full Thoughts

Middle age is so much more
Than wrinkles on our faces.
It's when broad minds and narrow waists
Begin exchanging places.

No Sweat

You know you're into middle age
When first you realize
That caution is the only thing
You care to exercise.

Sail On

Don't let your sedentary self
Become an oil tanker.
Grab the ropes and set full sail—
Instead of dropping anchor.

Know Sweat

The irony of exercise
Is seldom understood.
It first must make you feel real bad
Before you feel real good.

The Price of Perspiration

There's nothing quite like exercise
To put the glow back in your cheek,
To raise the body temperature,
To trim the old physique.

But the health club sent its bill today
And I just took a peek.
The blood is rushing to my face,
But I'm still feeling weak.

SPAtacular

The cost of gyms is killing me
With prices for the wealthy.
Instead of living to get fit—
I'm dying to get healthy!

The Era of Our Ways

People live much longer now,
Though it has come in stages.
We barely reached our middle age
Back in the Middle Ages.

Salt Shaker

I tried to give up salt again,
But I just don't know how.
My doctor says I'm doomed unless
I shake the habit now.

Heart Throb

My doctor said that walking
Would help improve my heart.
Walking out with bill in hand
Gave it quite a start.

Bored Walk

They say that walking's good for you.
To me it's not much fun.
I rarely have the time for it.
I'm always on the run.

Board Stiff

Working on the house myself
Was lots of fun until
The next week when I finally got
The chiropractor's bill.

Body and Soil

I've worked the weekend pulling weeds.
I'm hot and feeling foul.
Our garden still looks like a mess—
I'm throwing in the trowel.

Battle Fatigue

Push-ups, sit-ups, run-in-place,
Each night I keep a grueling pace
With bleak results I must divulge—
A losing battle of the bulge.

Healthy Kick Stand

My stationary bike is great.
I use it everyday.
It's where I hang my dirty clothes
When they get in the way.

Hexercise

The doc says I should listen
To my body — and I know,
But when I try to exercise,
My body just says, "No."

Health Food

We need to choose more healthy meals
And less based on their taste
Because the tasty food we eat
Just simply goes to waist.

No Weigh

The fastest plan for losing weight
And keeping pounds at bay?
Each time you pass the bathroom scale—
Just run the other way.

Fat Free Advice

Do not boast
Of losing weight
When you are on a diet.

Humility
Shall set you free—
If you should ever try it.

Nutty Professors

Scientists now all agree
That we are what we eat.
The study also shows that nuts
Have been their favorite treat.

Cultured Yogurt

They say that yogurt's good for you.
I'm skeptical and yet,
It is the only culture that
Some people seem to get.

Fat Chance

The odds against us staying slim
Increase each day at noon.
That's when they're set at three-to-one:
A knife, a fork, a spoon.

Hope Full

Hope is such a fleeting thing,
Though sometimes we deny it.
It comes and goes beneath our nose
Each time we try to diet.

Food for Thought

The irony of eating right
Is really quite profound.
The three square meals we eat each day
Often make us round.

New Age

Diets, spas, aerobic dance.
It's really quite a craze.
Everyone looks young again—
Just like the good old days.

Fiscal Fitness

To keep your health and business lean
Is easy once you find
They both depend on what you do
To trim your bottom line.

No Funny Bones About It

Laughter is the medicine
That can extend our pasts.
So keep your sense of humor
'Cause he who laughs, lasts.

VII. Sports & Recreation

Golfing Accident

Most accidents are blamed on fate
Except what man has done
When accidentally he makes
A lucky hole in one.

Commit Tee Meeting

Business deals are made each day
While playing games of golf.
The irony is they don't start
Till everyone's teed off.

Spare Me

My bowling skills are not the best.
It's baseball that I like
Because the game is easier
For me to get a strike.

Bowling Instructions

Bowling's based on timing,
On balance, skill, and grace.
Just put your best foot forward—
And don't fall on your face.

Boxing Lesson

Each champion must realize
When he is in his prime
That no one's ever won a bout
Against the hands of time.

TV Wrestling

A well-rehearsed and brutal show
That makes such little sense.
The only thing it really hurts
Is our intelligence.

Head Way

Soccer is a skillful sport
That has its own demands.
Although you need to use your head—
You cannot use your hands.

Cast of Thousands

Fishing tournaments are fun.
There really is no match—
Until you pay the entry fee
And realize you're the catch.

To Yacht or Not

A boat brings two great days of joy
As those who know will tell it.
The first is when you buy the boat.
The second — when you sell it.

Chess Nut

There's nothing like a game of chess.
It's patience at its height.
Where else can you just sit and take
All day to move one knight.

VIII. The Arts

Art

Art is undefinable,
A mystery of creation
Inspired by a pigment
Of your imagination.

Choice Art

The answer to the artist
Comes quicker than a blink
Though initial inspiration
Is not what you might think.

The Muse is full of magic,
Though her vision's sometimes dim.
The artist does not choose the work.
It is the work that chooses him.

Artfelt Emotion

The canvas glows with all your worth.
Your soul is gladly spent.
You worked the morning light with love
To your art's content.

Heart Art

The hand and eye must do the work
That earns the name of Art.
They take the viewer by the hand
And lead them to the artist's heart.

Art Show in the Park

The park is full of faces,
Some canvas and some real.
The landscape's full of landscapes
Where eyes can almost feel.

A microcosm skylight world
Where portraits hang from trees,
Where shadows brushed by tips of time
Are painting memories.

Staid of the Art

Outsider art is popular
Though many would agree
They call it that because outside
Is where it ought to be.

Art Eyes

Words can often cloud the truth
And veil themselves with lies.
That is why most artists like
To listen with their eyes.

A Good Impression

The water lilies of Monet
Drift upon a canvas bay.
A master of his profession,
He made a good Impression.

Music Matters

Music fills our lives with song.
It makes our spirits rise.
Dancing without music?
That's merely exercise.

Phantom of the Opry

Country music used to come
Straight from a country soul.
Today it's mostly city bred
And served with rock and roll.

All That Jazz

We wonder what they're playing.
We dare not interrupt.
Are they making music—
Or simply tuning up?

Jazz Magician

He turns his saxophone into
A satin hat and coat
And pulls a velvet rabbit out
Of every silky note.

Another Pointe of View

Our daughter is a dancer.
The ballerina kind.
Her posture is near perfect.
Her turnout is divine.

So when she joined the baseball team
Her mother said, "No way!"—
Until our darling daughter
Turned a double play.

Ergo Libretto

Opera is the highest art.
It's theatre, dance, and song.
It stirs the soul with drama—
Except when it's too long.

Of Chorus

A singer's voice is at its peak
Some say by thirty-five.
That is, of course, unless they're hoarse
And still, of course, alive.

Paint the Sunset

Paint the sunset with your eyes.
Sculpt the morning with your heart.
Brush your dreams with light and laughter.
Make your life a work of Art.

IX. Literature

Nevermore

The critics were unkind to Poe.
His life was short and sad.
His lust for drink led some to think
That he was Raven mad.

Waste Land

Eliot was under the delusion
That everything's an allusion.
Each line from T.S.
Requires a P.S.

A Thank You Note to Ogden Nash

Again I study and rehearse
Each measure of your pithy verse,
But since I fail to be as terse
I wish that you had done it worse.

Musery Loves Company

Poets mustn't smile.
It is their job, you know,
To brood about their life and times
Wherever they may go.

So if a solemn poet
Should offer you a rhyme,
Simply smile and say,
"No angst, I haven't got the time."

Literary Profits

Literary critics can
Find meaning everywhere.
They point out to the author what
He did not know was there.

The Happy Hypist

My publicist is satisfied
With clients who go far.
She is the one who likes to hitch
Her braggin' to a star.

Busted Bard

My editor just found the hack
Who stole a verse of mine.
His writing days are numbered now—
He lives on borrowed rhyme.

Re-Verse

The final draft upon the screen.
At last my poem's through.
A verse of only four short lines—
I rewrote twenty-two.

Stroke of Genius

The ups and downs of writing
Are simple, yet profound.
When inspiration comes along—
Get up and write it down.

Silent Echoes

A quiet rhyme upon a page
Is what a poet gives,
Gentle words whispered in trust
To see if memory lives.

Writer's Block

The path to inspiration starts
Upon the trails unknown.
Writer's block is not a rock.
It's just a stepping stone.

Poetry Is Not

Penned to the page
Waiting for us to admire.
It is only a lonely thought
Caught by tears on fire.

Double Vision

A writer's life is paradox.
It's more than what it seems.
We write of our reality.
The one inside our dreams.

Choice Language

A synonym is just a word
That we have chosen well.
Or one we like to use in place
Of one we cannot spell.

Suitable Language

Language is the dress of thought.
Your words wear every shade.
Be careful what you choose to say.
Your mind is on parade.

Book Stand

There's nothing like a favorite book.
There's little that can top it.
It's better than TV because
Commercials cannot stop it.

Royal Reader

I feel like a king whenever I read,
Especially while reading at home.
Without any hassle
I'm king of my castle—
Whenever I read on the throne.

A Novel Idea

A good book brings a smile
While TV brings a frown.
You never have to ask someone
To turn the volume down.

eBook

We stop and think—
No paper or ink,
A book that will not tear.

Who could have thought
That we just bought
A book that isn't there.

Light Verse

Simple language is the key
To open laughter's lock.
A gentle tap on humor's door
Is better than a knock.

Verse Case Scenario

I write a poem every day
And hope each one will sell.
I'll keep it up until I'm told
To curb my doggerel.

Oh What the Hack

Friends call me a poet
'Cause I can turn a rhyme,
But I am just a happy hack—
Living on bard time.

It Could Be Verse

My poet friends are puzzled.
They ask me why I do it.
"Why write this doggerel?" they chide.
They tell me to eschew it.

My dour band of brooding friends
Are such good solemn gents,
But I will live my life of rhyme—
As long as puns make cents.

Write Walking

If you should pass me on the street
And wonder what I said,
Please forgive my mumblings—
I'm writing in my head.

X. Science & Nature

Science Faction

Nature, it's true
Is full of surprises.
The sun doesn't set.
The horizon rises.

Sunsational

Wind and solar power.
We think they are divine.
Grandma used them long ago—
She loved her old clothesline.

Hay Feverish

Although I love this time of year
When blossoms have begun,
The pollen count is killing me—
This spring has over sprung!

Wysteria

Looks like grapes
And smells like roses.
Springtime's gift
To eyes and noses.

Spring Training

Mother Nature has a sense
Of humor that's divine.
Spring fever and spring cleaning come
Each year at the same time.

Pollen Nation

The world is turning green again.
The trees are in full-bloom.
Spring gets out her magic wand—
While we get out the broom.

Roadside Flowers

Flowers add so much to life,
A joy beyond belief.
The one that we could live without?—
The concrete cloverleaf.

Petal Pushers

They call it Fancy Potpourri,
But we think they have lied.
There's nothing fancy in it—
It's all just cut and dried.

Lawn Hot Summer

Once again I start to weed.
A task that's out of reach.
If crab grass grew among the crabs,
My yard would be a beach.

Summerize

The closet's full of winter wool.
The attic's heat is rising.
Back and forth with coats and shorts—
Our yearly summerizing.

Rain Checked

The weatherman said sunny skies,
A weekend dry and warm.
It's pouring on our picnic—
His usual brainstorm.

The Firefly

The firefly is quite a sight
Upon the summer wind.
Instead of shining where he goes,
He lights up where he's been.

The Brightest Planet?

Beyond the glow of evening stars,
We search for intelligent life on Mars,
But what would such a trip be worth
If first we found it here on Earth?

UFO or UAP?

Acronyms from outer space
Are full of mass confusion.
When will we see in real 3D
This optical illusion?

Plan It Earth

The sum of us will not survive
Though we are multiplying.
To save the Earth we all must stop
Our forests from dividing.

Land Grab

Mother Nature's losing ground
Despite our constant pleas.
Developers can't seem to see
The forest for the fees.

The Price of Emission

Poor old Mother Nature.
How could we be so rude?
Exploiting her for oil—
No wonder it's called crude.

Neil Armstrong

He was a model citizen
As honest as could be.
The only laws he ever broke
Were those of gravity.

Star Attraction

She taught him of astronomy.
They sat and watched the skies.
They fell in love and she became
His constellation prize.

Lighten Up

Don't criticize perfectionists.
They always leave their mark.
If Edison had not been one,
We'd all be in the dark.

It's All Relative

Albert Einstein
Had a relatively brilliant mind.
If you should doubt or even dare to
He could simply MC square you.

The Happy Pessimist

Earthquakes, floods, and fires,
Crime and apathy.
If cynics aren't happy now
I guess they'll never be.

XI. Technology

Virtual Reality

Computer games have changed our view
Of who we are and what we do.
Beware the headset that you don.
It may be one that turns you on.

Old Software

Today computers do the work
Of all our daily thinking.
The only problem now is how
To keep our brains from shrinking.

PC or Not PC

It's not the latest programs
That confuse my new PC,
It's just that it's compatible
With everything by me.

My Cussed Computer

My cursor's frozen on the screen.
My mouse is stuck like glue.
Another glitch and soon I will
Become a cursor too.

Computer Eyes

Eight hours staring at the screen
And I can hardly think.
My Mac is still computing,
But my eyes are on the blink.

Garden of Eden

See the wonders of the world.
The Earth, the sea, the sky.
Don't let a little screen become
The Apple of your eye.

Deus Ex Machina

Geeks of greed, we build machines,
Robots with computer screens.
We rush to run a losing race,
Creating things to take our place.

Know Joke

Technology cannot replace
The jobs of working folks
Because computers cannot laugh
At all the boss's jokes.

Phone Tag

Each time we try to call our friends
We know just what it means.
We're forced to spend our precious time
Talking to machines.

Listen Hear

Robo calls are such a pain.
Who falls for this baloney?
Although they try to sound so real
Each one still sounds so phony.

Bar Coded

Those little lines beneath our names
Are everywhere we look.
Computers meter out our lives
And read us like a book.

No Cause for Alarm

My new alarm clock bit the dust.
It's in a broken heap.
It kept on going off each day—
While I was still asleep.

XII. Faith & Inspiration

The Art of Start

Don't search for inspiration
When you have a task to do.
Just start your work and you will see
That it will soon find you.

Blind Faith

Our vision is not limited
By our own worldly lot.
The mind and heart can clearly see
That which the eye cannot.

In Sight

Close your eyes and look inside,
A mirror shines within.
To find where you are going,
First see where you have been.

Religion

Some want it simple
With clear certainty
While others like searching
The vast mystery.

Reformation

What makes a sermon memorable
Is not the time it took,
But how the preacher used his Muse
To prophet from The Book.

Moving Sermon

The preacher and the realtor
Are much alike by far.
They'll tell you there's a better place
To be than where you are.

The Power of Patience

Life is full of challenges,
Chores to keep us guessing,
Until we learn that we can turn
Our burdens into blessings.

Rare Dessert

Love is not for only those
Already at the feast.
We often need love most of all
When we deserve it least.

Earth Bound

More souls are buried in the Earth
Than all who walk above.
Earth is but a tomb we share—
So fill your life with love.

Conscience

It leads us toward a truer path.
It answers many whys.
It shakes the truth out of its sleep
No matter where it lies.

The Right Angle

Solutions to a problem
Are easy to untangle.
Just find the right approach
And use the old try-angle.

The Right Touch

A thoughtful word, a thoughtful deed,
We never lose the knack,
For kindness is a boomerang
That always comes right back.

All the World's a Stage

Every day's a brand new play
Each time you do your part.
A smile on your face will cue
The song within your heart.

Secrets Are Gossip

Secrets are gossip about to escape.
They take a deep breath then exhale like a drape
That suddenly opens and there in the sun—
A window of streaks that's never undone.

The Mighty Secret

The secret caused a mighty stir
When someone finally told it.
The tongue does not weigh very much—
Though few can ever hold it.

Pair Annoyed

The paranoid is one whose lip
Is constantly in pout.
He begs for you to let him in—
But keep the others out.

Light View

There's nothing gray about the truth.
It's simply wrong or right.
Shadows disappear from view
When we stand in the light.

Jacob's Ladder

No matter how high you climb.
No matter how low your crawl.
The rungs on the ladder really don't matter
As long as your faith doesn't fall.

The Unbeaten Path

Climb beyond the beaten path.
Look up and never stop.
With every step you take you make
A new path to the top.

Dalai Lama

The only thing
That makes him worry
Is why the world's
In such a hurry.

Proof Positive

Two things that will never lie,
That always will prevail:
The smile of a baby—
And a puppy's happy tail.

Tears of Joy

Emotions flow in many forms
Like rivers toward an unseen goal.
Be grateful for your tears of joy—
They soothe the gardens of the soul.

Real Quack

One who spouts out sour words
Is called a sourpuss.
One who spouts out platitudes—
A boring platypus.

Mind Bending

Conversations exercise
The mind once they've begun
While gossip only shows us how
To exercise the tongue.

Light Show

When traveling in foreign lands
Or places that you know,
A friendly smile lights the way
No matter where you go.

Living in the Past

History teaches much to us,
Though dwelling there's unpleasant.
Give up the baggage of the past
And open up the present.

The Present

Live your dreams before they fade
Like blossoms on a bough.
There isn't time for everything.
There's only time for now.

The Sell-Us-A-Dream Prophecy

These New Age books give us new hope
That life need never end.
While skeptics say it's just a fad
Of who knows where — or Zen.

Soothsayer or Truthsayer?

Prophecy or intuition,
Both misunderstood.
Either way they're still a guess
That finally made good.

Life's an Illusion

Nothing is as it appears.
It's only as it seems.
Reality does not exist—
Except within our dreams.

Dream Land

Each night we leave this world of ours
And venture out past shooting stars
Into a world beyond our bed—
The universe inside our head.

Reality Check

The facts of life come to us all,
Arriving unannounced.
Reality's the only check
That no one ever bounced.

Double Departure

You can't take it with you,
And you'll also find
After all the funeral costs—
You can't leave it behind.

Charles Ghigna is a poet, children's author, and nationally syndicated feature writer. He is the author of more than 5000 poems and one hundred books for children and adults ranging from the 1990 Pulitzer Prize nominee *Returning to Earth* to the popular children's book *The Father Goose Treasury of Poetry for Children.* His books have been published by Disney, Random House, Scholastic, Simon & Schuster and others. His poems for adults have been published in *Harper's, The New Yorker, Rolling Stone, The Saturday Evening Post* and *The Wall Street Journal.* His poems for children appear in *Highlights for Children, Cricket, Ranger Rick, Humpty Dumpty, Jack and Jill, Spider, Ladybug, Babybug, Caterpillar, Children's Diges*t and *The School Magazine.* He served as poet-in-residence at the Alabama School of Fine Arts, instructor of creative writing at Samford University, and has received fellowship grants and various awards and recognitions from the John F. Kennedy Center for the Performing Arts, the Mary Roberts Rinehart Foundation, the Rockefeller Brothers Fund, the National Endowment for the Arts, and the Library of Congress. A popular speaker at schools, colleges, conferences, and libraries, Ghigna has spoken at the American Library in Paris, the American International Schools in the Americas in South America and Alaska, and at other events throughout the U.S. and overseas.

For more information please visit
CharlesGhigna.com

www.ingramcontent.com/pod-product-compliance
Lightning Source LLC
Chambersburg PA
CBHW031559110426
42742CB00036B/247